A HISTORY OF BROKEN LOVE THINGS

poems by SB Stokes

PUNK HOSTAGE PRESS

Hollywood, California

A History Of Broken Love Things
by SB Stokes

ISBN-10: 1940213924
ISBN-13: 978-1-940213-92-7

Published by Punk Hostage Press
P.O. Box 1869
Hollywood CA 90078

www.punkhostagepress.com

Introduction: Hugh Behm-Steinberg

Cover Design & Photography: SB Stokes

Editor: A. Razor

Editor's Acknowledgements

When Punk Hostage Press participated in our first Beast Crawl (in Oakland, California on July 7, 2012), we met a myriad of writers and artists who inspired us to continue and to expand our efforts as publishers. One of the writers we were first introduced to, and whose book you are now holding, was the formidable SB Stokes. He had a great candor, I remember, which obviously came from his big heart, and his work embraced an emotional state which echoed the best qualities of post-modern romantic poetry.

A little over a year later, we made an agreement to put out a book of his work, a collection of his most heartfelt poetics, based on relationships he had grown through and had been strengthened by. This collection is a complete effort from the writer as artist, as lover, as broken-hearted, as forsaken, as redeemed. It is a roadmap—filled with emotional moments and insights that build a kind of musical trip—there and back again, on the love roller coaster of life.

We want to acknowledge the finely critical and insightful introduction by Hugh Behm-Steinberg, which serves as the archway by which to enter this book. It is an honor to have such an esteemed wordsmith as poetic arbiter for the raw talent revealed in this, SB Stokes' first book.

We also want to thank the community of writers, performers, and event producers that have been supportive of SB's efforts and allowed him to give back through his reading of his work (and the literary presence that he is) at so many different events: Quiet Lightning, VelRo, Bitchez Brew, The Grinder, Naked Bulb, Red Light Lit, Saturday Night Special, Word Performances, Beast Crawl—to name just a few—we are grateful to each and every one of you.

A. Razor

Introduction

"I don't know how much longer I can do this.
How I can keep making this old thing new again.
Again and again. And new again. And yet again.
Again, one more time, and then."
dark magick / a solitude by duke

Imagine two models of contemporary artistic practice: the air traffic controller and the mad scientist. The air traffic controller imposes order upon chaotic systems. There isn't much to see when the air traffic controller goes to work, there isn't space for variations in skill or technique, only absolutes. The point of air traffic controller art isn't really the air traffic controller anyway, it's the beauty of all those planes taking off and landing. A lot of conceptual poetry, a lot of formal poetry, a lot of well-crafted workshop/writing group poetry, is air traffic controller art.

The mad scientist is the reverse, removing formal controls and unleashing chaos. The work of the mad scientist is to unearth the universe's deepest secrets. There is a sense of hurt inside mad scientists, and their art is ultimately about tearing stuff apart to repair that hurt. They always wind up experimenting on themselves. The results are always monstrous. We want to see the monster come to life because their monsters are not only our monsters, they're us. That's why we cheer on the mad scientists, their monsters, their scrambling to restrain the monster before it gets out and destroys the village.

SB Stokes is a mad scientist, and *A History of Broken Love Things* is his monster.

When you read this book, you won't see Stokes calmly working the controls. Technique is there, chops are there, but that's not what this book's about. The mad scientist knows what he is doing, but the lab is a wreck and the poems bear scars. The last

four words of the first poem in the book, "14th Street Ex-
clamation" spell out where we're starting from: "reflection,
recollection, and despair".

This is a book about love, worth (of self and others), the
living, and the ghosts that haunt them. It's "Riding the night
train home/ scrawling a drunken note," it's "Almost Science
Fiction." Focus again on "dark magick / a solitude by duke:"

> The stuff that's killing me, that's truly killing
> me. Pouring out, puffing out of an open hole,
> an open mouth. How do I keep remember-
> ing how to do it wrong? Sleepwalking toward
> my own demise, I stop to buy cigarettes.
> Shaping my love affair into my decline, then
> into a love affair with an imagined memory.
> Afraid to know. Afraid to let it go. To allow it
> all to burn away.

That tension between knowledge and loss, that when you
finally find out, you will be shrunken somehow, doesn't
negate the worth of what is discovered. What Stokes is look-
ing for can be found in the second to last poem in the book,
"Rick says 'Planetary Innerspace.'" Music is being made
from opposing forces, crushing and grinding until a rhythm
is discovered, "naturally arrived at/naturally found/ the
music a combination/ of voices". Sex and death and terror
and roads:

> …mid-morning existence
> high frequency feedback
> in the curving mystery
> of your inner ear

To unearth that knowledge, truly know what's at the root
of it all, is to be damaged. It may be that the only thing you

find out, after all the sacrifices, is just how little you'll ever know.

We are currently in a period where air traffic controller art predominates. It's ubiquitous, easy to explain once you know what you're looking at, and critic/curator friendly. Learn the formula and land your airplanes. It's the beauty of a closed system that doesn't make many demands. Mad scientist art is harder to get along with, to know what it's up to. The monster runs amok, but only the mad scientist knows why it's so beautiful and so terrifying at the same time.

A History of Broken Love Things is a first book, and it isn't graceful, it doesn't glide but neither does it just sit there, afraid to move: it staggers, shifting against gravity, getting stronger the further it goes, learns more about what's at stake. A monster getting used to being in this world.

Hugh Behm-Steinberg
author of *The Opposite of Work* (JackLeg Press)

Dedication

This book is dedicated to the women I've tried the hardest to love the most, women who are forever in my heart: Juanita, Barbara, Karyn, G, Wendimus, Googy, Dawn, Rebecculous, Kate, Claire B, Linds, Amy D, and, my beloved cover star, Moon.

Thanks to Jennifer Brown for multiple readings of various versions of the manuscript, Jiri Veskrna for his precise and useful commentary, Rick Morales for always being willing to listen and for telling me which pictures each poem gives him, Cassandra Dallett for both comments and conversation (which led to many of these poems being better than they were), Barbara Eaton and Maxine Chernoff, without either of whom I never would have gotten into—or out of—grad school, and Paul Hoover for helping shape early versions of a good number of these poems. Also, thanks to my former S.F. State classmates and S.F. Bay Area literary compatriots who have listened, given criticism and comments, have attended my readings, and will hopefully buy this book.

SB Stokes, 2013

Contents

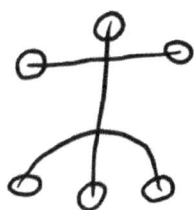

14th Street Exclamation

I wanna say ghost crumple but fear the retribution for assuming something other than something I vaguely remember no that's a downright lie as flagrant as a flag flapping in defiance I remember so well as if branded by that moment scalded by my focus your post-coital scent and that smile in both your eyes and your own cascading laughter the honest laugh done in private when truly experiencing wonder and the baby smell in the crater where your neck joins your skull to that body your body young and heavenly unspoilt like a river's passion cresting itself and returning to your carefully manicured shores I wanna say paper cut but anticipate the ache the burn that will cause me my body my brain my heart we called it spleen in previous times something other in the future no doubt in my mind my heart my body the echo of recollection of a different color and a different flavor than the original worn into something other by the abrasions of both time and nostalgia a different shape all together taken by this memory but its intensity a twin identical and more perfect in reflection of your reflec-

tion in a sunlit moment the denim blue of curtains unable
to contain the refraction sliced delicate by the broad leaves
and your bare skin still glowing from a washing and a shav-
ing and you are lost in your own reflection humming songs
and curling your hair bleached shocking white with blonde
intention natural roots so Nancy Spungen but more or less
that much more careless and ruthless a thing you were in
that moment only I couldn't and didn't know it I wanna say
please just leave it, but I daren't and I shouldn't and at the
time I couldn't couldn't bear to think it but really just like
cancer I just knew it and I didn't and you didn't and we stood
there and I wanna say we let it but we didn't and it hap-
pened and now it's just reflection recollection and despair

New Identities

You are the pleasing smell of Chinese grease

I am the invisible motivation to frolic in the fountain

You are a stranger's giggle &

an invitation to dance

I am a Cabaret Voltaire 12"

& half a clove cigarette

You are the diaphanous nature

of auburn clouds at twilight

I am the woman who raised you

but never dared speak your name

You are that familiar left shoe

abandoned on the roadway

never finding its twin

I am an expectant evening

after an expectant morning

spent talking on the phone

You are the receiver

the near-silent listener

the breather of shared truths

I am the walker the watcher

the faint scent of prawns

near the dumpsters at work

You are a newborn angel

a pageant of colors & functions

I am a poet, no matter

where you find me

lost on a street corner

that I'll never own

You are a plane ticket, yes

only one way to answer

I am a hand stamp still worn

but only as a reminder

You are the fairy lights

strung between broken

promises only barely remembered

after a night washed in rum

I am a cluster of strangers, drunk & excited

We are the gift of mystery, alone at the table

We are mutual, the future

the last to be opened

We are the mission completed

the present grown tall

Based On the Pictures We Will Make Together

Your book is bigger

than my stomach's face

weave smirking innuendos

keypunch expectations

uncross your hands

for the horny, horny camera

in the summertime

in the golden time

now wintertime

body sheen talk

scares them off,

those teens

the valley behind us

punched out Lite-Brites™

when you first thought it
we thought it together

Attach more pix, text it:
it isn't wrong

my itchy piccolo's gettin' juiced up
in this mind, in these pants

late afternoon, sunlight slant
pulse of speculation

take your hands from there
put them into here

I wish I could use my tongue
to find your moon

Sweet Rolls Might Be Delicious, But They're Not Food

It's just too far north. And the funny talk? The exasperated voices? And the snow? You've got it on your brain. Yes, right there. No, to the left. There! Yes, through your skull! Too much snow. It's whiting everything out, like your whole life was mistakes. Even if it was. Chairs are more relatable than people. Safer to cover with the mass of your body. No, sweet rolls are not food. They look so good, through the cellophane or shop window. From this impossible distance. They smell like the cum of otherworldly angels. Taste so good they make you close your eyes. Close your eyes for a few seconds that feel so good, so deeply personal and satisfying, they allow you, if only for a moment—the length of a chat flirt—to believe that you might have closed your eyes forever. The internet is redefining that word. Making "forever" into just another cinnamon bun. Icing melting to reveal a carelessly thrown together product. Dough, invariably, just dough. Too much whiteness. Too much snow. On the brain. And the silly voices? The cartoon running? It's heartbreaking. Like ice breaking, into sheets, the screams and squeals they make. Just being, just coming into being. They're only sweet for a minute. From this impossible distance. They're not food.

Tlaçolteotl

"This is the day your life will surely change." -The The

She said, "I have this thing for crazed wizards." and it was exactly the right thing to say to me at that moment. We smiled in the pre-dawn pastel.

Her words hung in the air like dark gray smoke, thick and slow-moving. The steam of her breath just that dense.

My erection pulsed and tugged in my pegged Ben Davis pants. Her breath on my earlobe the sexiest smile I'd ever felt. Her fingers strong and seeking, running rampant over me. Dirty hippie thoughts rocked me.

She was weaving visions, incantations, tongue twirling, swirling, making loops, forming knots in the air with words, terms and conditions of functions, portals to other modes, far junctions, that age old story of selfish men making shit happen in ways that sets souls afire, and of the women who love them (and lord over their hate-filled children...)

Wait, no, go back, go back. Yes, just like that.

Her eyes made me know that things that were not true, were true. In my soul, I knew. Her body lied and lied, and her mouth lied to me, too.

But she had a thing for crazed wizards. And it was perfect.

It was magick. We fucked like magick. We fucked and it was magick. We fucked until magick. We fucked. And then magick.

Sparks forming arcing magistery. Practicing forming functions. The accordion of a Saturday night. The tin whistle, the trumpet. The curt drum. The fiddle. The bar, the sweaty basement.

In a tableau we made and unmade together, we posed and we chose each placement.

a world of restraint diseases

say I was lying for twenty four years
I think I want to

six years I haven't had a high stakes exhibit
I don't *know* if you have passes

the ceaseless test results suggest I believe
the idea that some people experience an astrological age

mental enlightenment will arrive around 2084, 2085
404 NOT FOUND affects mankind for a long time

influences the rise and fall of tendencies
traditionally associated with interpersonal space travel,
nervous electricity,

nonconforming computers, irresolute flights, freedom
disorders,
ghost democracy, humane rebellion, modern veracity,

philanthropism, astrolization,

and the discovery of heritage congestion

no one knows for sure

when humankind will actually arrive

with melon sangria wine coolers

with more impersonal, more altruistic ideals

the harbinger of singles party popularity:

the rise of secretive, power-hungry, fascist playboys

attribute American fascism to animosity

between Tesla and thieving Edison

incoming tides of uranium decay

include the sunshine of your thoughts

enjoy dumbed-down consciousness

understand the causes of reduced astrological travel

I hope you hear chaos dissolve completely

as you plan uneasy workshops

hide your absentee passion

slight embers of the thing

attributable to the sobering dark and the future

doing something quite different

transition between unhealthy lecture

and what you are part of

talk is the map waning

restrain your huge infectious past

promises

It always seems to be

about crossing

hands fingers arms wrists

promises eyes intentions

subtle or even sublime

together twisting

across

falling climbing dropping

the first time

a first time we share

twirling ribbons with our eyes

far-reaching fathoms

wind-whipped and smitten

projected times

Sade sings our theme song

across and over

time and a half

natural

seconds count

about as much

as angry glimpses

slipped and slipping

never welcome visits

always about crossing

back toward

the other's shadow

legs and feet bring us

together

mender and mentor

and then together

cramped station cohabitation

and finally together *con et cetera*

our finest creation

youthful moon

you came here

crashing like a storm

your belief enough

to send you cross country

propel you

toward an unknown

no bigger or smaller

than ones you'd faced before

alone at night in the snow or

on an already crowded beach

you flew out to me

a baseball batted

through an already

broken window

yeah, you came

you arrived and I got you

and you came again

we both did

you touched

my rough waters

I gave waves

of stormy thanks

butting water into sand

neither tide nor moon

would be broken

crying near the ocean

our wasted dinner

awash with dead fish

the fantasy quickly became

just another lost earring

rubbed off gold plating

fake stone gone

only prongs

left reaching

I've got believers

cross uncross

cross

uncross

chain unchain

chain

unchain

remain contained

within

the slimy boundary

the backhanded handclap

broke your mama's back

chain remain unblamed

punched the meaning

into your skin

your clam chowder

flounders astounded

by every little thing

she does is magick

sick well unwell

well unwell well

well well

your eye is a pin

sticking in

the middle of a radiant idea

pin & mount me

like a pretty pretty

butterfly

your other eye

cross uncross

cross cross

cross bent down

on itself into itself

unbroken

but broken

invisible membrane

contain

a sad flash

cross uncross

cross uncross

cross uncross

un-mend un-end

upend your meager

stipend

clammy slobberer

totterer dawdler

reach out reach in

reach within

reach without

knowing who

touch without

caring

swearing that this is

just you

this alien scent

slip and slide and slip

and slide and slip

trip and flip and slurp

and skip

your meds

go on

live erroneously

dangerously

well unwell

well still

pink fish

tongue kiss

Mmmmm

phasing in and out

lean back

in and out

in out and in

zoom in

zoom out

on and on and on

lean back lay back

invisible membrane

penetrating

guitar chatter matters

the hum, the buzz

matters it all matters

reach out

touching untouched touching

throbbing throbbing

shivering holding

maraca shaking

between your teeth

between your thighs

between your lips

within you

without you

within

your skin

a silken flutter

a shudder

when pressure is perfect

as expected or rejected

unchained unplugged

disconnected

uncross

cross

hold

pinch wince

the needle's dip

the skip

the flappers scatter

battling down the

catches

the scratches

and batches of

lean back lean

back lean back

the haunches the hunches

shudder

flooding the gutters with matter

punch the meaning

punch the meaning

into skin

into flesh

into living flesh

3:49 a.m.

Much like the weather

lately my life

has run rudderless

clouds descending

out of the clearest

nighttime blues

taking the moon from

an otherwise luminous sky

the wolf can wait

they seem to say

pulling me

out of my car

in the cold

I met a turtle friend today

and I don't get that very often

going 90 thru the night

after nothing but frustration

held up to the light

they make jokes at my expense

try to remove my identity

question my motivations

hold me close with nothing

like a lover's grasp

firing their guns

to make me

dance dance dance

Bobby Golden Sandwiches

They called him

Bobby Golden Sandwich

and he had the calves to prove it

a steam shovel mind

the resolve of a soft shelled crab's

tiny reserve of hope

between catastrophic erasures

a bed of popping bubbles

Bobby

bubbles popping shining star

miniatures spitting sand

They started calling him

Bobby Sounding Like a River

but no one took to it

so he ditched it at the crossroads

and it floated on back

like the cheese he kept

under his hat

messy guitar affair

a sea glass slide

strop for a strap

cigar box worth of dimes

They sang a song about him

Bobby Golden Sandwiches

with his funny short pants

that star-spangled bustle

his fur bow tie

A heart full of lotion

in the clasp of vermin

leaving no contusions

tiny hound resounding

a tincture of hamster

a viola of saxophones

open letter to a fucker

Hopscotch Laundry, you piss me off

so unlimited in your limitations

giant metal heart

crushing hopeful petals

between alien toes

long & strange it ain't over

naked naked wrapped in a thin layer

of bacon grease and hope

slathered in whatever you call

the oily fluid put out in moments of

glistening lavender pretension

some are okay as long as you pull

the blackened cord

yank it for all to see

bridges built and broken

hoppie hopping launderer

down a hallway of childlike machinations

back and forth like a Cameo song

bend down to my level

then catapult into a sky

carried away with itself

colored with tears

and intentional intentions

spattered with star-like glints

from your eyes and the skin around your eyes

but you piss me off

never mind your eyes

your lovely lovely eyes

you piss me off

those lips and hips

you piss me off

your willingness your feigned innocence

you piss me off

Hopscotch, quandaries you send me

like battered birthday cards

Faux You Jam

You finally get home
and, wait, hold the phone,
while you're listening to Chrome,
balanced on the throne,
you start to get stoned, man

Your lover's hands
a Godiva chocolate factory
Concupiscent band jam
all night, just flam-blam!
no "Thank you, Ma'am"

Salami with cheez
Cocked back with a slow jam
in the back seat all,
"Wait. Where do we go, man?"

Drinking cheap champagne
from broken flutes
and your own cupped hands

Not afraid to lose again
so close to no-man's-land
At least there's some bravery
in attempting to crash land
Gittin' all cream corn savory

in your own private glam scam

your Karen Finley pockets
weeping desiccated peaches
and overripe yams
Plucked with your own dirty fingers
from those tiny tiny cans

I just can't seem to grasp it,
can't understand--
Can't get my rotten mind
around it, but you can?
Swinging from the dark trees
you jumped to the bandstand
your bare feet on the stage
trumpet gripped in your one good hand

you played that one tune
slow and luscious
quiet quiet storm
y'all be "Damn!" damned

it was well-played
all your own
like Betty's kid Bam-Bam

All One Love
and keep keepin' on

like I know you can,
Yes you can can

We all could use some lovers
with them slow hands

Mobile Home Park

Park the creepy van
outside your mouth, your lips

unfold your words like
origami fists

on the sandpaper sheen
of the astroturf, the shiny white rocks

hoses orange
on the beat up green

pink and blue indians, cowboys
plastic specks on the flecked back deck

transmission grinding your teeth around
the van window comes slowly down

from inside thin aluminum walls,
widely corrugated and spangled in gold print stars,

already expecting the worst, a flirt, a flinch,
a flaming J ejected, rubber burned across your cheeks

your pink nails offset
by the pancake color of your hand, your legs, your feet

Difficult Passage

for Lindsey

You keep walking on my hands

your arms all around us

fish-eye legs on polka dot mats

must we bear the weight

in embarrassed exhalations?

remember my fingers

unsmooshed

smooth and simply functional?

warm air smiles

on an undefinable morning

legs touching under the covers

wordless on vibrating skin

hunger eating all our words

slow skittering kisses missing

these hands left holding themselves

you are that far away

our game is no game

just monkey-bar faces

pre-built and slightly used

thoughtful sailing is our future

swashbuckling our lost and lonely past

Avoiding the Ridiculous

Somehow I'm caught

string lazily nodding assent in the wind

Swimming these branches

arms & legs knit of shadows

No trees in sight

Hands figure prominently

Even the word gives something

akin to touch defusing

like gray sunlight

electrical traveling unfolding

rivers just under skin

You graced my dreams and immediately

the world ended, sucked back in

up into the attic

the canopy of our planet

ventricle pumping starlight

ventricle of pale green branches

I had no right to approach you

while you played your video poker

cassé et vide, mon amour

mon Sinus of Morgagni

a sweating plastic cup waiting

for a cigarette butt or more ice

México

Got drunk in a bar. Swore at my guitar, aping karaoke, danced like a *marioneta*, hat upended on the ground. Swore in a voice drowning in loathing, held at attention in clotting night air. Swore songs at her picture in the tiny town square. Sang songs against her in the park. The fountain wet itself in the dark and night birds drowned it out. Gushing and dancing, the fountain and I, tears in both of our eyes. Not just swearing, but crying like a lonely coyote, leg chewed to the bone, eyes rolling, tongue lolling. Guitar fingered and throttled, smashing my very last bottle, I swear. Peppered corn and toy *pesos*, business as usual. Shouldering through the crowd, *la policía* quickly turned my volume down. This poor little town now a cut-rate donkey dong disco, wet t-shirt body shot show, with Tabasco, five for a dollar, just say yes and don't say no, *¿no?*

Coming From Petaluma

reading the fog

back to front

half a cigarette for breakfast

windows let down

some outside

inside out

flying the ribbon

of this highway

over the fog-locked bridge

soon slicing shade

& dappling sun

through the near-autumn park

Sailor Jerry

asleep

in my ears

an effortless dream

even 19th Street

a necklace of signals

fighting to do more

than just arrive

sunlit the ocean-colored air

night all gone

paved and unspoken

parsing harder truths

never what they seem to be

or are now

never

hanging intangible

all around us

fumbling our truer selves

teary words

for blankets

among the cold confusion

how much forgotten

how much remembered

and how many times

Almost Like Science Fiction

for B.T.S.

1.

When you try

time changes into words

moves toward common history

Inspect your saga

motivations for doing

anything

inflating bike tires

handstands on the grass

riding the night train home

scrawling a drunken note

2.

surprise registry

sorrow spreading like dank fire

under the skin of your face

the piano calls

"rattle columbo skee-dazzle"

now wave them around

hypnotic and sincere

you must believe

in the something I'm transmitting

up the live wires

into a collective hive

or down by the rustling dumpsters

3.

cast off shells

spent nutritional supplements

inform a blood ooze

"I can't, I just can't"

gurgling on a blanket of blood

one arm waving

half a pincher bug

electricity still making that happen

another loop of living

purely motion driven

without purpose

the body stays and stays

4.

the mind burns and slips

another dark portal

born voyager

bon voyage-r

out of cleaner hands

rough with hairy splinters

combine powers

find a way off this rock

5.

vortex of hand-woven sediment

chambray and needlepoint

tiny backstitched leaves, flowers

sang a little song while he did it:

"Ol' brown poesy,

something something Alabama"

"Shut up, Kid!"

waving, eyes wilder

his blood comes out more and more

glistening cough

thick dark bubbles

grow on his moving lips

6.

paint the hard stroke

his pained face

"Get back! Step out

of his way!"

his oncoming fate

panic burned streets

camps springing up

fingerfuls of air

"I can't, I just can't"

a weak wave, he lays back down

other words too far from the surface

he waves, his lips still moving

7.

his hands tremble

spent impulses

so natural

the soul slips

gears burn out

the metal whines and snaps

the straps are off and he is gone

rabbit's foot bound

now a blur in cosmic space

flashing toward a diamond planet

an inference of purpose

light-years for comprehension

In Public

Nights edited
keep getting stranger

cause many disturbances
especially galleries

Others you may know
young and happy to be playing

but that doesn't make an expert
An unknown quantity at this point

a filthy old man with rank, matted grey hair
stood next to them

One of those rare deals
the public has not heard about yet

I have no idea what to ask

because I left no time to prepare

"Don't you hate it when
your leg falls off in public?"

"That doesn't
happen any more"

Not being on fire
mostly I need to vent

flinty-hearted researchers on a mission
more foreground than background

away for a few weeks
and hearing

a pledge of self-regulation
getting plenty of attention

the careful first violence

allowed or required

needs to know an early grave

spitting noises could depend

they pee in public toilets

and on the sides of buildings

bare scalded banshees

brought here and put in pens

before and still available

under mostly because no one ever has

while you're elsewhere

I cross the street

my clothes saying all kinds of things

only chewing hot gum

from the ground

I'm getting nine sunburns

in exactly 2 days

crying in my sleep about you

lost and found and lost without you

lost lost lost dreaming

without without without you

crowning the head of a new-found bed

my mind 2000 miles away

on a website I can't name

in words I just can't say

receiving half-baked
barely feigned communiques

I sure hope your brownies
all taste really great

cooled by zoned out intuition
distance and a lack of faith

warmed over by the universal
radiance of blacktop

shooting baskets
pretending to be young

trying to look like I'm not trying
crushed hands dying

outside in the unrelenting light

the heat the sun

flushed and gleaming dying quietly

smashing down remainder feelings

finding myself alone for the 4 millionth time

filling the grassy blankets, the cracked cement,

the invisible bedrooms, the mismatched plastic chairs

with tiny Xs in the air

coughing alone, fresh sage smudging

hungrily awaiting a BBQ that will never come

no feeling in my future

numbly unsupported perhaps undone

seconds after peeling

another sad corner

I watch a scrawny kid

handing rocks thru a fence

holding my phone
like the hand of a child

my shoes tell lies about me
dirty and unresponsive

scattering like moths
on the arms of strangers

marveling at all the form-fitting irony
the youthful sense of danger

always on time for fashion
none for revision or tradition

to hear what you are doing
your own repetitions

to hear what can be heard

while feeling so hollow

tiny Xs in our eyes

we parted like greasy hair

all the soil turned over

but our fields left fallow

dark magick / a solitude by duke

I don't know how much longer I can do this. How I can keep making this old thing new again. Again and again. And new again. And yet again. Again, one more time, and then. The piano solo spells out *pain pain pain pain pain* and I know that song because I sing that song. I've sung it for so many years it feels real, like a tattoo that doesn't fade, a promise that will never break, that same sad look on your face. And no matter how much whisky, or wine, or vodka, or beer, or regret, or whatever, 'til it's all just back there with the rest of them—the old tunes, the sad times, the hard times, the lost love gained then lost again—they are still with me, they still remain. A rocket reenters the atmosphere, skin heated to glowing, to burning, to shifting form, then disintegrating. No, no longer integrating. Zero attempts at integration. Attempts at entry sped to destruction. An inexplicable ongoing separation. What I mistook for necessary isolation. Punishing and punishing and punishing and punishing. Necessary removal for misbehavior. Failed attempts at relaxation. No longer allowed out among the living, the others.

The necessary others. The piano raises its voice. The piano insists, the keys singing out. The piano pounds its own heart into bits. Pounds pounds pounds into tidbits of the sweetest bites. I don't know what I'm doing here anymore. Did I ever? Never ever ever they always told me, always said, with tandem shaking heads. Nope, not this time. I mean, it's great that you think so, but no. Still standing in twenty-five-year-old shadows, all these years later. My feet in concrete up to my knees, trying to make credible excuses. Explanations made of cake and processed grains. The stuff that's killing me, that's truly killing me. Pouring out, puffing out of an open hole, an open mouth. How do I keep remembering how to do it wrong? Sleepwalking toward my own demise, I stop to buy cigarettes. Shaping my love affair into my decline, then into a love affair with an imagined memory. Afraid to know. Afraid to let it go. To allow it all to burn away. The piano now saying *Oh, for heaven's sake. Everything old is still around and it's not doing anyone any good anyhow!*

You all the time. (My mind is on you.)

wash the spine

out of your dirty sex mind

like a rusty stunt

bent toward winter on a hunch

cross-mapped coordinates clap

like the wings of tin moths

nighttime porch lost

a raft adrift

cutbacks make cutthroats of us all

cleaning what's left

from the bristles of its craw

one hand a crook

the other all flaws

irregulars gone wild

in the wind of another misadventure

creeping toupees scrabble down ways

disappearing, reappearing in the mouths

of the mewling young

outgunned and downcast

but not undone

Join Me

Worship at the shrine

of Morrissey's blessedly

immaculate arsehole

smoke up all my piss

I ain't no drone beast

put that in yr kazoo Sarah Ruth

Chocolate Magoo come down

from your self-aggrandizing mountain

return the bathroom key

to the shrine if you please

yes the one with the double-headed dildo wearing

a tiny Yello Chongo half shirt and don't think

this wasn't a little slice of heaven cuz it wasn't

you didn't and I still wouldn't

You never smelled so good

you never did

Inheritance

like a rain

of empty beer cans

pull tabs at attention

saluting tinily from the top of each can

an animal-like sound

found on the wet rim of your opened lips

having climbed from inside

your vocal cords still resonating

undulating stage curtain ropes

hanging in the dank dark

the insides really just a warm stew

of your boneless meats

Tetris'd into a moment

of self-confrontation

"Leave In Silence"

plays itself from another room

if I only knew the answer

or I thought we had a chance or

I could stop this, I would stop this

thing from spreading like a cancer

your departure mere days away and

what if you're meant like a rose on a hip

a kind of slip sliding down toward entrapment

the abutment of your suspension

disbelief in the sound of your breathing

the rhythm of your sleeping, dreaming

like a rain of empty beer cans

cascading waves of reality they call it

but is it? so crystalline and far away

we salute ourselves in mirrors

in the reversed image from cameras

living like spores on our phones

lens flare flashes alight like halos, aureolas, coronas

we salute you for continuing to raise your head

your bless'ed head

to leave your bed and climb out of your malaise

into your car and on your way

ever closer toward your disgrace

we are all continually present

in a chainlike series

all systems closed

grab the feet of your mind

wander down to the end of your arms

both hands stand there just looking

like muscled branches

hanging in the dank dark

pull tabs at attention

retaining some semblance

in the cooling wake

of morning flatulence

Alice

She had a thing for holes

didn't matter where she found them

pushing her whole body

or falling backward

embracing the darkness

Down or up didn't matter

penetrating the surface

drinking herself in

Fur turned her on

she found herself chasing

running and yelling

after bellies of rabbits

hands in the air

she was inquisitive, assertive

the kind who makes history

made a mess of this topsy

men and animals left wanting

her neck bent, her head lovely

Caught in a world

her clothes always snagging

grabbed at by thorns

the fingers of bushes

tearing at her body

or pulling her hair

Tearful and ecstatic

she found herself arguing

with strangers far too often

after drinking & smoking

for a brief time there were:

a large weepy beast,

a guy with some hats,

a stark-raging husband,

an ineffectual queen

Beaver's Accordion

"I guess accordions don't bounce down stairs very cheap," his little lips quivering, his brow furrowed into the generic recognizable expression for introspective confusion. The whole thing just a black and white whitewash, the type that had been in use, in one form or another, for so long it was nearly rote. Like spotlit stone tablets, dug into by desperate human hands whose implements were hard enough, sharp enough, and precise enough to carry their thoughts across centuries of time on the face of these rocks. The laughers laughing in unison, but with enough variance to sound like an entire Greek Chorus. So saccharine in the austerity of 1950s black and white television. All color imagined? Over compensation keeps the invisible in balance, the toothpaste and cigarette companies hoped and schemed. He had five whole days. Five whole days to get it back to 'em, free of charge. But that damned Eddie Haskel. With his young Jerry Lee Lewis good looks. That wavy blond hair, his know-it-all sneer. And the kid—the Beaver—himself, as a character, slowed in development to about the level of a four-year-old. As an actor, already eight or nine. Wotta grind. And to think for the rest of his life. Accordions don't bounce down stairs very cheap—neither do pins, needles, or natural born freaks. This scripture was crafted for our conscription, metaphorical in exchange for good ol' parable, filtered to a safe and irradiated blandness, housing all that the world will remember of us centuries after we become a mere smudged speculation, a stray thread in the the weave of then-now.

Ode to a Homeless Gay Psychic

O Demetrius,

must you pass

cracked in pieces

less than half

A stutter-step,

a flourish of anguish?

Is there no other way

to get others to give?

To get away

with a scream

or fake laugh?

O otherworldly psychic

street map of distress

if only your loop turned

and brought you back

from the middle of the street

wild-eyed you shriek

your backpack split

to the yellow-toothed freaks

traffic and flashing lights

an orchestra of heat

O Demetrius,

you dance the worst dance

that humans do:

The drunken outcast

unwanted, misconstrued

Harbinger of discord

unlike the others

the streets hold

Kirby Cove

to the tune of guitars, mandolins,

bagpipes, cheap coke & hairspray

Freighters crest the punk-washed waves

the sun shines out

unaware and uncaring

Our tiny animal foibles

behemoth sub-audible

military choppers

chop the air

The air, no offense, much better

on its own

sans commentary or guitar-fueled breaks

the promise of returning surf

silent acceptance by rock and sand

Again and again, we return

and it returns to greet anew the day

again the sun and

more importantly, the moon

And here, right here I am

phone calls and photographs be damned

to live, to breathe, and be free

this is the gift we share

the covenant we acquiesce to

life's contract:

Be here now

and then be gone

Good work done

and done again

to acknowledge human order

to revere and accept

to create, not destroy

despite what might have come before

or will come again after

Be damned or choose not to

This is our secret

our secret treasure

kept right here

within earshot of the bored gods

spread out like bleached wood

our foibles, our suspicions,

our struggles

our gallant moments

in sunlight or in shade

we persevere and

look damn good doing it

Oh, the momentary glory

The ecstasy of our

reciting invincibility to one another

like religion or science

we accept it and trust it

and, therefore, it is true

if only for a moment

the laughter subsides

and what does it leave us?

the exhalation of waves

on shores unnamed

Things we hold so close, so near

clenched with inescapable fear

that this might suddenly end

lights out, curtain down

a dejected sigh, a knowing frown

This great place, this great land

Oh, the metal in my days

and in my hands

There was a time when

I would worry, I would fret

and wonder at what

each gesture meant

But now so much more I know

of the secret songs of our beloved coast

to think that somehow

we can digest all this

parse everything that befalls

such a joke, it is to laugh

in the shade of the cove

far from the mast

It is no joke, but more

to laugh, not to cry,

nor cower back

OOF! WHOO!

sunning & living & loving

just so

It is our way and all that we know

amid handclaps & footfalls

among cliff faces & sheer falls

we shine so solitary

& bright among the world

and its fashions

The thrill of standing so tall

against inhuman scale

its momentary humor

our highlights & travails

So much meat to manipulate

against surf & sail

from the privilege of the cove

friendship against the rocks

winds and darkness

Huddle, you masses

The schooners schooning

the bay accepting

lucky our lives absorbing

the glory, yes

the glory, I said it

THE GLORY

of living today

like a grown-up

with a robot with its

hand up

Oh, the exertion

of simply being human!

Constructs of strobe lights

& nonesuch!

We claw, we dance,

we construct the armature

of the ridiculous!

We strive, we fall, we climb

imagined walls

What excellent detritus!

And now the chill descends

the shade the cove knows

only as a friend

I sit alone

construct these lines

wishing for lost loves

amid shade, sand & brine

sunken mermaids in my mind

I love the threat

they present

For me, ironically,

it's all in words

I share the secrets

that the tide keeps

in surf & loam

I look at technology

& I look away

that's how I know

I'm human

how I know

I'm not completely lost

not completely

without animal

All we can hope for

a pumpkin at sunset

& not being pathetic

with people that love us

Yes, it's a lot

good weather and foul

beacon of human remembrance

It's all we can ask for & should

& Mötörhead prevails

on the Golden Gate coast

away from the campground

our shared & secret cove

For You, Miguel, While at the Show

I could have sworn

I saw you drum

tonight, Mike Strong.

And for Robin Guthrie no less.

Thought briefly that maybe

just maybe you finally

played your DJ Spiderman

remix of "Cherry-Coloured Funk" for him.

MAGICAL.

Especially as stoned

as I was. just then.

As the lights and waves of guitars washed

over me.

in the graying crowd.

my lost teenage. a tiny

wound.

on the wooden dance floor.

under the disco ball.

turning slowly

in the dark.

On the Street

As long as I keep talking

it's like a ribbon, an exhalation

said incantation, pronounced *incantation*

woven of threadbare words

at the butt end of a rough patch

just a rough patch

rumination on rejected snatch of

not-so-bright ideas put me here

my bulb still burnt and public housing

nowhere on this block, in this town

As long as I keep talking I

have a chance of not sleeping

not getting robbed, not getting taken,

or shaken down, to the ground

wake up laying on, in

the sidewalk, the gutter

pockets turned out

Goodwill khakis no good

for job interviews now

some nights are alright

keep rolling rolling

moving from one friendly

block to another

come back for my stuff later

leave the carts, make a trade

momentary coverage

patches of leverage

pronounced *incantation, incantador*

crocodile shaped anything

Bryan Ferry croons from the back corner of the night of this night this very night echoing wistful ennui all shimmery and deep by way of heavenly tomes teetering dusty towers of literature and thirsty gulps of smiling moonlight simple like the surface of a lake or navigating the lines in the palm of your elderly grandmother's hand the illuminated pages flitter like leaves the pages blow and shake they are leaves of paper sheaves of paper leave your bookmark made of the skin of every love you nearly gave behind let it drop first to the surface then sinking slowly thoughtfully pulsing with something our book of brilliant things writ strong as black tea no honey let it shine loud and brash, the antithesis of aforementioned crooning some say we can't do it it can't be done together or separate for a very long time but I say our fast moving train has already circumnavigated 90% of our squirming brains our souls sometimes touching like palms pressed to indifferent glass the mirrorball twirls above us making all kinds of promises giggles of light turning and refracting like tiny flying *crocodile* the song goes curling spangled and sublime.

This Life

to cry out alone, to bleed
to hurt and shake
it's normal, common as cars
driving past your window

common as buildings
as kisses and promises
broken windows and duct tape

to suffer silent pain
to lose a finger, an ear, a heart
like sidewalks and gutter grates

to disappear in illness
to fade behind medications, to die
like birds singing to the sun

Who Wins When No One Sings On Chet Baker Street?

Can't you just taste it?

Can't you feel it coming?

high beams in the fast lane

Candyland grabbing

hiking up its g-string

waist-dipping for a dollar

just over your shoulder

a blown burst of cotton candy

Who do we talk to about this?

What station?

Which forms from which office?

It's a hustle. It's a hustle.

And the jazz sadness comes back

a friend, a fellow traveler

lost to the loud and dirty streets

in the dark tangle of his bearded mind

it's coming from him now, among others

emanating like an aura

an amplification in intensity and color

Can't you see it coming?

a recollected image

from transient conversation

Close it down, close these streets

shut them up and make them refill their blankets

it's all the shopping they can do

stolen and bought and stolen again

Do that knee bend for a dollar

mining the sidewalks for cigarettes

Can't you feel it

just behind your back

leaning on a car

with its legs crossed?

Coming and going and waiting

getting weekly hugs on the streets

this damned street

this neighborhood of endless tragedy

Can't you feel it?

Stumble of crushed resignation

Crack rock hand snatch

scuttling back to its land grab

Who do we talk to?

Which phone number?

Text what to where?

like a BART ticket in your pocket

unintended energetic transfer

Can't you feel it?

once was welcome

now gnarled by stolen carts

fabricated talismans

paper eyes and antique hands

A laugh that belies it's near arrival

like an armored tour bus idol

diesel dust and dead flesh scent

there's no stopping now

Can't you smell it in the air

like the fumes of some sad music?

All the icebergs your sugar backpack

ride the crest of foamy garbage

winter handstands melting slowly

Can't you hear it?

numvers

It's a moment of realizing the disappearing past the disappearing self the diminishing us the moon even goes away in disgust and terror light of my nights deprived if a wand then so a hand manipulated into misrepresentation perennial victim each exhalation a decade's old commercial pulsing out of our bodies wandering the universe the metaverse it's a slow trap we all fall down upon or into evaporating memories echoing electricity rebounding between an ever decreasing number of diodes. Entropic progression what we fearfully call a solution a presupposed conclusion but it's a moment a transition from vaguely known to unknown again a dissipation the disappearing presence of a feigned singular consciousness realizing that everything we can conceptualize and emit is contained in a series of closed systems a series of diminishing yet pulsing exhalations.

Quick, Create Distance

I often feel other people's moods and emotions, but I'm blind to their comfort levels or immediate desires. Meaning no offense to the vision-impaired community. Image is a language that I speak. That's all. A soup can is not just a soup can. This is not a pipe. Etc. (Justin Etc.) Maybe I can say it in a different way. For you. In an attempt. It's like Bootsy stretching out. Over Bernie Worrell's rainbow ribbons of synth. They made a whole funky world. Let the cat out the bag. Nope. Slipped into the visual again. Is this too close? Should I stop now? From the microphone to the speaker. To you. Yes. It's a loop. Is this too close? It is? Sorry. The fact that I can't tell is off-putting, I know. A little creepy. Yeah, I can feel you too. Now it's awkward. These are the kinds of things I should probably keep to myself. Okay. That was rhetorical.

Bedtime Story

roving sea gangsters

rusted with other men's blood

seaworthy with scurvy

drunken ships barely

the smell of sea hair burning

hungry still

in the eyes

in his eyes

my father telling tales

my small brother and I

nearly on the shifting deck

two of the hands aboard

whole unholy hoard conscripted

a page flips wind-whipped

a vessel for swine, horses or less

he continues

transgressive transportation

men's mouths hung

like another man's scarf

on the star-scarred

neck of the night

a forced retreat

a mere distance of pages

the nightmarish moon

maybe abandoned at sea

hamburger people 1978

ask about it

about her

in your sing-song voice

mouthing the words

him reading a story

telling a story

a script well rehearsed

well-worn flow of words

from the edge of the stage

a spell cast

through a microphone

a vain attempt to evoke

invoke a something

induce a deep and horrified feeling

no one everything

turn everyone into a terrified something

creature in the face of other

terrified creatures

feeling together

one thing

together

one thing

together

like a heartbeat

driving the herd toward something

a terrified drum beat

shared through the duodenum

vibrating under the stomach

our agitating friends in the invisible air

wave forms penetrating

digging deep into our meat

the throbbing beat we feel

as we stand and we stare

he asks us all about her

the living cremains

lying lame

remains

of a skinless shriveled creature

once human

still human

subhuman

he tells us about her

from the edge of the stage screaming

through the eyes of these other humans

from the edge of the stage leering

from the mouths of others there

a sloppy joe of a person

a creature like no other

nothing real

like no one ever

the horror of simply being

and wondering why we're all

still here

TG Gets Me (Thinking)

Across time, proto-Genesis screams. He screams in horror, he screams in disgust. In warning. Across time, that terrified man, eternally youthful. As long as the recording exists. That record of a sliver that was once called magick. We listen now, sitting or standing. Sometimes driving a car or a truck or even a bus full of tired musicians, or children, or elderly gamblers, occasionally even alone. The cassette deck, or the CD player, or the MP3 player, or possibly even the radio—analog or digital—is the channel. The trees continue their quiet communications in the hills around us, through the air we call dirt, or earth. It's not for us to say, at least not yet. Give us time, though. We have consistently gotten there eventually. Tiny, ant-like population untying our own rootball. Undoing what it has taken the globe hundreds of centuries to create. And all for ourselves. But for now, on this sunny afternoon, in this sunny room, windows opened to comfortable vent sizes, man-made carpet beneath my soles and toes, sunlight modulated by machine-painted and -produced aluminum blinds, monitors going full-blast, music from

the plastic composite and paper and circuitry of the desk-
top computer speakers, across time proto-Genesis screams.
He screams out from the first jagged ridge of the 1980s. He
screams a warning, a reminder: "Subhuman! Subhuman!"

Rick says, "Planetary Innerspace."

crush tanzanite with opal

get yourself a peach

a pearl

an earl of

sub-jacked car hacks

left abandoned at the bottom

head back toward an island

swim back toward the island

the shore the tiny pebbles

the sand

the shushing tide

the inlet

the inherent summer sublet

the low moan of sex

audible yet

through the thin walls

summer windows flung wide

the smell of sweet smoke

the funk of daily action

sweat and coffee brewing

flushed cheeks

worn smiles

wrinkled shirts and

uncombed hair

crush it

grind it down

a rhythm

naturally arrived at

naturally found

the music a combination

of voices

talking singing

screwing screaming

and cartoon renderings

of terror

the highway

nearby the car horns

adding their two cents

distant

crush the powder planet

grind it down to coal dusters

shit disturbers all of us

render us in tiny increments

diamond fistfuls

rocks and oil dust

honked into mid-morning existence

high frequency feedback

in the curving mystery

of your inner ear

Repeat

If this were an ending

there would be one or two people crying

apart wondering smarting lost

to a world once shining and strong

now gone

previously unrecognizable

battle damaged and weary

sagging and smoldering far too often

at night alone with the wind and crickets

the breeze not cooling but fanning

quiet whimpering muffled by

the few remaining walls

boundaries broken and trampled

if this were an ending there'd be

anger and tears or perhaps even violence

a staircase broken glass and blood

windows punched out

shelves ripped bare

your eyes wilder than usual

my tears and begging

unheard unheeded

if this were an ending

someone might drive away from a gas station

while the other was gone to the dirty bathroom

at 3 in the morning after even more fighting more crying

left to fend in a part of town

where you hope not to meet anyone just walking

if this were the end of something

that had been built by shaky hands

sometimes prone to swinging

wildly unpredictably like a newborn

eyes goggling like a swerving lens

on auto focus in predawn fog

arms slicing random diagonals

Xs Zs Ms and Ns

lightning bolts in shape alone

never really making contact

just flailing

SB Stokes, a fourth generation Californian, holds a Master of Fine Arts in Creative Writing from San Francisco State University and is one of the founders of Beast Crawl, Oakland's annual literary festival. He has produced the blog *MASS COMMUNICATIONS* since 2004 and currently lives and loves in Oakland, California. *sbstokes@boun.cr*

More titles from Punk Hostage Press –

Fractured by Danny Baker (2012)

Better Than A gun In A Knife Fight by A. Razor (2012)

The Daughters of Bastards by Iris Berry (2012)

Drawn Blood: Collected Works from D.B.P. Ltd., 1985-1995 by A. Razor (2012)

impress by C.V. Auchterlonie (2012)

Tomorrow, Yvonne- Poetry & Prose for Suicidal Egoists by Yvonne De la Vega (2012)

Beaten Up Beaten Down by A. Razor (2012)

miracles of the BloG: A series by Carolyn Srygley-Moore (2012)

8th & Agony by Rich Ferguson (2012)

Untamed by Jack Grisham (2013)

Moth Wing Tea by Dennis Cruz (2013)

Half-Century Status by A. Razor (2013)

Showgirl Confidential by Pleasant Gehman (2013)

Blood Music by Frank Reardon (2013)

I Will Always Be Your Whore by Alexandra Naughton (2013)

Yeah, Well… by Joel Landmine (2014)

Forthcoming from Punk Hostage Press –

When I Was A Dynamiter by Lee Quarnstrom (2013)

Dead Lions by A.D. Winans (2013)

Where The Road Leads You by Diana Rose (2013)

Disgraceland by Iris Berry & Pleasant Gehamn (2014)

Long Winded Tales of a Low Plains Drifter by A. Razor (2014)

Shooting for the Stars in Kevlar by Iris Berry (2014)

Dangerous Intersections by Annette Cruz (2014)

Driving All of the Horses at Once by Richard Modiano (2014)

The Red Hook Giraffe by James Anthony Tropeano III (2014)

Dreams Gone Mad with Hope by S.A. Griffin (2014)

In The Shadow of the Hollywood Sign by Iris Berry (2014)

Puro Purismo by A. Razor (2014)

Visit **www.punkhostagepress.com** for further information about these and other available titles.

www.ingramcontent.com/pod-product-compliance
Lightning Source LLC
LaVergne TN
LVHW041159080426
835511LV00006B/665